Little Boy Blue

Illustrated by Stuart Trotter

Little Boy Blue,
come blow your horn.

The sheep's in the meadow,
the cow's in the corn.

4

Where is the boy
who looks after the sheep?

He's under a haystack fast asleep.
Will you wake him?

No, not I!
For if I do, he's sure to cry.

7

Little Boy Blue

Little Boy Blue,

come blow your horn.

The sheep's in the meadow,

the cow's in the corn.

Where is the boy

who looks after the sheep?

He's under a haystack fast asleep.

Will you wake him?

No, not I!

For if I do, he's sure to cry.

8